STATE PROFILES

ARIZONA

BY RACHEL GRACK

BLASTOFF!
DISCOVERY

BELLWETHER MEDIA • MINNEAPOLIS, MN

Blastoff! Discovery launches a new mission: reading to learn. Filled with facts and features, each book offers you an exciting new world to explore!

BLASTOFF! UNIVERSE

GRADE K

GRADES 1-3

GRADE 4

This edition first published in 2022 by Bellwether Media, Inc.

No part of this publication may be reproduced in whole or in part without written permission of the publisher.
For information regarding permission, write to Bellwether Media, Inc., Attention: Permissions Department,
6012 Blue Circle Drive, Minnetonka, MN 55343.

Library of Congress Cataloging-in-Publication Data

Names: Koestler-Grack, Rachel A., 1973- author.
Title: Arizona / by Rachel Grack.
Other titles: Blastoff! discovery. State profiles.
Description: Minneapolis, MN : Bellwether Media, Inc., 2022. |
   Series: Blastoff! discovery : state profiles | Includes bibliographical
   references and index. | Audience: Ages 7-13 | Audience: Grades
   4-6 | Summary: "Engaging images accompany information about
   Arizona. The combination of high-interest subject matter and
   narrative text is intended for students in grades 3 through 8"
   –Provided by publisher.
Identifiers: LCCN 2021019663 (print) | LCCN 2021019664 (ebook)
   | ISBN 9781644873748 (library binding) |
   ISBN 9781648341519 (ebook)
Subjects: LCSH: Arizona–Juvenile literature. | CYAC: Arizona. |
   LCGFT: Instructional and educational works.
Classification: LCC F811.3 .K64 2022 (print) | LCC F811.3 (ebook) |
   DDC 979.1–dc23
LC record available at https://lccn.loc.gov/2021019663
LC ebook record available at https://lccn.loc.gov/2021019664

Editor: Christina Leaf   Designer: Laura Sowers

Printed in the United States of America, North Mankato, MN.

TABLE OF CONTENTS

THE GRAND CANYON

SOUTH KAIBAB TRAIL
GRAND CANYON

On a warm spring morning, a family hikes the South Kaibab Trail of the Grand **Canyon**. They trek down the winding path. Each turn offers a new peek at colorful **buttes** and jagged walls. The children's eyes widen as they look over the steep edge at the trail below.

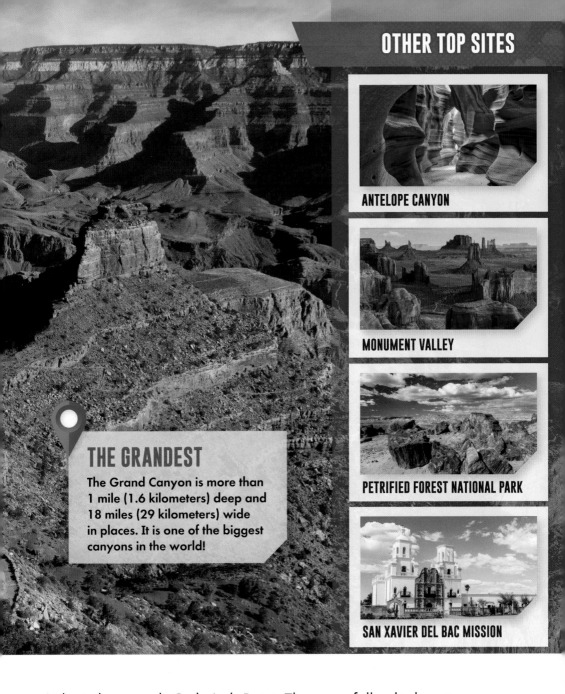

ANTELOPE CANYON

MONUMENT VALLEY

PETRIFIED FOREST NATIONAL PARK

SAN XAVIER DEL BAC MISSION

THE GRANDEST

The Grand Canyon is more than 1 mile (1.6 kilometers) deep and 18 miles (29 kilometers) wide in places. It is one of the biggest canyons in the world!

At last, they reach Ooh Aah Point. They carefully climb onto the rocky lookout and gaze across the canyon. The view is breathtaking. Jutting peaks and carved **bluffs** twist as far as their eyes can see. Sunshine lights up the canyon walls in brilliant shades of purple, red, and orange. Welcome to Arizona!

WHERE IS ARIZONA?

UTAH

NEVADA

COLORADO RIVER

FLAGSTAFF

CALIFORNIA

ARIZONA

SALT RIVER

PHOENIX ★ SCOTTSDALE
MESA

TUCSON

MEXICO

NEW MEXICO

Arizona lies in the southwestern United States. It covers 113,990 square miles (295,233 square kilometers). Arizona is bordered by Utah to the north and New Mexico to the east. Mexico lies to the south. The Colorado River creates Arizona's jagged western border with California and part of Nevada.

The state capital, Phoenix, is located in south-central Arizona. It lies on the Salt River. With around 1.7 million people, it is the largest city in the state. Tucson is the next-closest in size. It is surrounded by mountains in southeastern Arizona.

ANCESTRAL PUEBLOAN VILLAGE

People first came to Arizona at least 12,000 years ago. Many other groups later **settled** throughout the state, including **Ancestral** Puebloans. Later, the Navajo, Apache, and other groups came to the area.

CASA GRANDE RUINS

Until about 1450, the ancestral Sonoran Desert people lived at the Casa Grande Ruins site in Coolidge, Arizona. The *Casa Grande*, or "Great House," is one of the largest prehistoric structures in North America!

In 1539, European explorers came to Arizona in search of gold. Later, Spanish priests established **missions** there. In 1752, Tubac became the first lasting Spanish settlement. The area became part of Mexico in 1821. The United States later gained control in 1848. In 1863, the Arizona **Territory** was formed. On February 14, 1912, Arizona became the 48th state.

NATIVE PEOPLES OF ARIZONA

TOHONO O'ODHAM

- Original lands around the Salt, Gila, and San Pedro Rivers in southwestern Arizona
- Around 28,000 in Arizona today

NAVAJO NATION

- Original lands in the Four Corners area of Arizona, New Mexico, Colorado, and Utah
- Around 173,000 living in Navajo Nation today
- Also called Diné

APACHE

- Original lands in east-central and southeastern Arizona and parts of Colorado, New Mexico, Texas, and Mexico
- Around 15,500 on the Fort Apache Reservation and around 10,700 on the San Carlos Reservation today
- Also called Ndee and Inday

HOPI

- Original lands in northeastern Arizona
- Around 9,000 on the Hopi Reservation today
- Also called Hopituh Shi-nu-mu

Arizona has two main regions. The Colorado **Plateau** covers northern Arizona. Deep canyons cut through the high, flat land in this region. The Colorado River created the famous Grand Canyon there. Mountain ranges such as the Gila Mountains run through the middle of Arizona. The **Basin** and Range Region covers southwestern Arizona. It includes the dry Sonoran Desert.

COLORADO PLATEAU
GRAND CANYON
BASIN AND RANGE REGION

N
W E
S

SONORAN DESERT

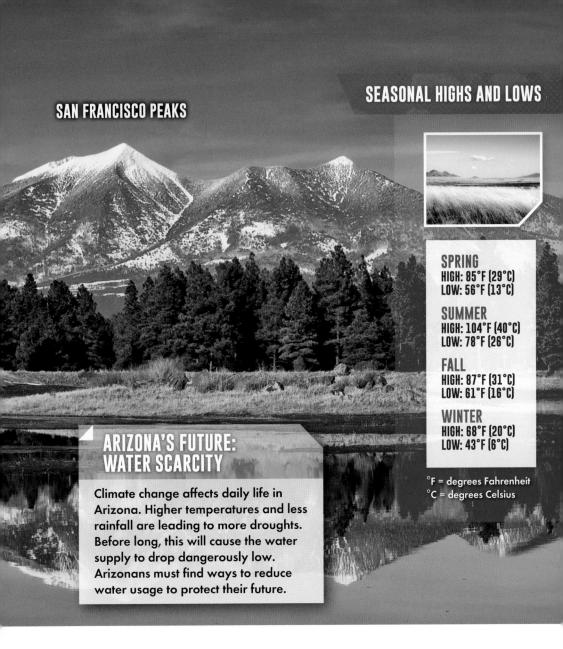

SAN FRANCISCO PEAKS

SPRING
HIGH: 85°F (29°C)
LOW: 56°F (13°C)

SUMMER
HIGH: 104°F (40°C)
LOW: 78°F (26°C)

FALL
HIGH: 87°F (31°C)
LOW: 61°F (16°C)

WINTER
HIGH: 68°F (20°C)
LOW: 43°F (6°C)

°F = degrees Fahrenheit
°C = degrees Celsius

ARIZONA'S FUTURE: WATER SCARCITY

Climate change affects daily life in Arizona. Higher temperatures and less rainfall are leading to more droughts. Before long, this will cause the water supply to drop dangerously low. Arizonans must find ways to reduce water usage to protect their future.

Southern Arizona is generally warm year-round. Little rain falls throughout the year. Arizona's central mountains are cooler. They get snowfall in the winter. The Colorado Plateau is dry with hot summers and cool winters. Arizonans look out for **flash floods** and sandstorms.

11

CALIFORNIA CONDOR

Desert bighorn sheep climb rocky cliffs in northern Arizona. Sharp eyesight helps them spot stalking bobcats and mountain lions. California condors soar overhead. They search the Grand Canyon for dead animals to eat.

ROUND-TAILED GROUND SQUIRREL

In the Sonoran Desert, jackrabbits perk up their long ears, listening for coyotes on the prowl. Speedy roadrunners snatch up lizards, tarantulas, scorpions, and cactus wrens. Rattlesnakes curl up under bushes and in rocky caverns. They wait to strike passing ground squirrels or quails. **Venomous** Gila monsters bask in the hot sun. They are the largest lizards in the United States!

GILA MONSTER

BLACK-TAILED JACKRABBIT

DESERT BIGHORN SHEEP

📍

BARK SCORPION

More than 30 types of scorpions live in Arizona. The bark scorpion is the only one with a deadly sting!

GREATER ROADRUNNER

Life Span: up to 8 years
Status: least concern

greater roadrunner range = ■

LEAST CONCERN	NEAR THREATENED	VULNERABLE	ENDANGERED	CRITICALLY ENDANGERED	EXTINCT IN THE WILD	EXTINCT

More than 7 million people live in Arizona. It is one of the fastest-growing states in the country. Most Arizonans live in **urban** areas, especially around Phoenix and Tucson. Some people live in **rural** areas or on ranches. Twenty-two Native American nations live in Arizona. **Reservations** take up more than one-fourth of its land area.

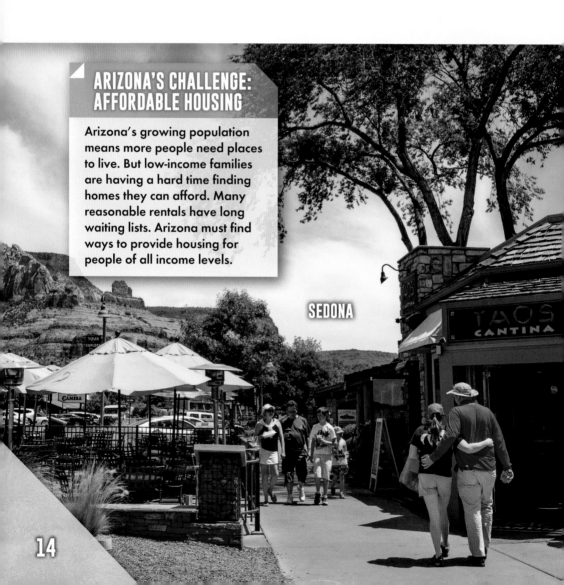

ARIZONA'S CHALLENGE: AFFORDABLE HOUSING

Arizona's growing population means more people need places to live. But low-income families are having a hard time finding homes they can afford. Many reasonable rentals have long waiting lists. Arizona must find ways to provide housing for people of all income levels.

SEDONA

FAMOUS ARIZONAN

Name: Emma Stone
Born: November 6, 1988
Hometown: Scottsdale, Arizona
Famous For: Academy Award-winning actress who starred as Gwen Stacy in *The Amazing Spider-Man*, as the voice of Eep in *The Croods,* and as Cruella de Vil in *Cruella*

THE CROODS

The majority of Arizonans have European backgrounds. But that may change as the Hispanic population grows. Today, over 3 in 10 Arizonans are Hispanic. More than 1 in 8 Arizonans are **immigrants**, mostly from Mexico. Other newcomers are from Canada, India, the Philippines, and China.

Located in north-central Arizona, Flagstaff was officially founded in 1881. But the town actually began earlier. On July 4, 1876, settlers nailed a U.S. flag to the top of a ponderosa pine. This inspired the city's name! During the 1880s, railroads and lumber helped the city grow. Today, **tourism** keeps the city booming. Around 5 million people visit Flagstaff every year.

The slopes at Arizona Snowbowl resort offer skiing, snowboarding, and tubing. People go snowshoeing or cross-country skiing on mountain trails. Hiking is popular in summer. Some people enjoy concerts and fine art at Coconino Center for the Arts.

DARK SKY CITY

In 2001, Flagstaff became the first International Dark Sky City. Its clear, clean sky and limited night lights make it a perfect place to stargaze!

SNOWSHOEING

COPPER MINE
MORENCI

Arizona was once known for its five Cs. They include copper, cattle, cotton, citrus, and climate. These are still big industries. Arizona leads the nation in copper mining. Beef cattle and dairy are important farm products. Lettuce, hay, and cotton are, too. Arizona grows much of the country's cantaloupe, honeydew melons, and lemons. Its sunny climate attracts many visitors. **Service jobs** in tourism and other areas make up a large part of the workforce.

Manufacturing is another big industry. Computer equipment and electronics are some of the state's most important products. Arizona is in the top five states for aircraft, spacecraft, and even missiles.

INVENTED IN ARIZONA

TREE RING DATING
Date Invented: early 1900s
Inventor: Andrew Ellicott Douglass

PLUTO DISCOVERED
Date Discovered: February 18, 1930
Discoverer: Clyde Tombaugh

PAWSENSE
Date Invented: 2000
Inventor: Chris Niswander

TAMALES

Many Hispanic families make tamales around Christmas. But street vendors in Arizona sell these tasty snacks year-round! They are made of *masa* corn dough filled with seasoned meat and steamed in a corn husk. Navajo tacos are another state favorite. These use **fry bread** instead of tortillas.

SONORAN HOT DOGS

Sonoran hot dogs are wrapped in bacon. They have Mexican-style toppings such as pinto beans, fresh salsa, jalapeños, avocado, and sour cream.

The Sonoran Desert grows foods unlike anywhere else. Prickly pear cactus fruit is like candy! It gets used in jelly, tea, and syrup. Mesquite flour, made from the seed pods of mesquite trees, tastes sweet and nutty. It bakes into sweet breads and pancakes. Spicy chiltepin peppers also grow wild. They add a kick to salsa!

PRICKLY PEAR CACTUS FRUIT

EASY CHIMICHANGAS

8 SERVINGS

Chimichangas are fried burritos. This famous food was first made in Arizona. Have an adult help you make them!

INGREDIENTS

1 fully cooked rotisserie chicken, shredded

1/2 cup salsa

1 tablespoon chili powder (optional)

1 1/2 cups cooked Spanish rice

1 15-ounce can pinto beans, drained

1 1/2 cups shredded Colby Jack or cheddar cheese

8 10-inch flour tortillas

oil for frying

sour cream, guacamole, and salsa for serving

DIRECTIONS

1. Fill a medium frying pan with 0.5 inches (1 centimeter) of oil. Heat on medium high.

2. In a bowl, mix together the shredded chicken, salsa, and chili powder, if desired.

3. Spoon rice and pinto beans in the middle of each tortilla. Top with chicken and shredded cheese.

4. Fold up each tortilla.

5. Fry the tortillas, two at a time. Cook for about 3 minutes or until lightly browned. Carefully turn the tortilla, and cook another 3 minutes.

6. Drain the oil from the tortillas on paper towels.

7. Serve with sour cream, guacamole, and salsa.

HORSEBACK RIDING

With around 300 days of sunshine each year, Arizona offers many outdoor activities. People enjoy horseback riding and hiking through mountain forests and meadows. Lakes and streams are popular fishing and camping sites. Winter snowfall creates excellent ski slopes. Indoors, people enjoy listening to Arizona's orchestras. Families visit the Phoenix Zoo and OdySea Aquarium. At the Heard Museum, visitors learn all about Arizona's Native American **cultures** and art.

Arizonans love their sports teams! Fans pack stadiums to cheer on Cardinals football and Diamondbacks baseball. Arizonans also cheer for the Phoenix Suns and Phoenix Mercury basketball teams.

SPRING TRAINING CAMP
Fifteen Major League Baseball teams come to Arizona for spring training each year.

NOTABLE SPORTS TEAM

Phoenix Mercury
Sport: Women's National Basketball Association
Started: 1997
Place of Play: Phoenix Suns Arena

TUCSON RODEO

The Tucson Rodeo in February is one of the largest festivals in Arizona. More than 200,000 people show up for its kick-off parade. A week of rodeo events includes bull riding, steer wrestling, roping, and barrel racing.

DAY OF THE DEAD

In early November, many Arizonans celebrate the Mexican holiday *Dia de los Muertos*, or "Day of the Dead." They decorate altars called *ofrendas* and honor the dead with music and dance.

Arizonans honor the Native American art of hoop dancing at the World Championship Hoop Dance Contest in Phoenix each February. All age groups compete, even kids and toddlers! Every September, the Navajo Nation holds a fair in Window Rock. Fairgoers experience Navajo culture through food, performances, and crafts. Throughout the year, Arizona is a fun state!

WORLD CHAMPIONSHIP
HOOP DANCE CONTEST

1752

Tubac becomes the first lasting Spanish settlement in what is now Arizona

1881

Lawmen and outlaws have a shootout at the O.K. Corral in Tombstone

1539

European explorers come to Arizona searching for gold

1848

The Mexican-American War ends and the U.S. gains control of much of the Southwest

1912

Arizona becomes the 48th state

1919

The Grand Canyon is named a national park

1942

Navajo men, now known as Navajo Code Talkers, join the Marines and create an unbreakable code to send radio messages in World War II

1981

Arizona judge Sandra Day O'Connor becomes the first woman Supreme Court Justice

2001

The Arizona Diamondbacks defeat the New York Yankees to win the World Series

1936

The Hoover Dam on the Arizona-Nevada border is completed

Nickname: The Grand Canyon State

Motto: *Ditat Deus* (God Enriches)

Date of Statehood: February 14, 1912 (the 48th state)

Capital City: Phoenix ★

Other Major Cities: Tucson, Mesa, Chandler, Scottsdale, Flagstaff

Area: 113,990 square miles (295,233 square kilometers);
Arizona is the 6th largest state.

Population

7,151,502
(2020)

STATE FLAG

The top half of Arizona's state flag is red and yellow beams. They look like a colorful sunset for Arizona's western location since the sun sets in the west. The beams stand for the original 13 American colonies. The bottom half is solid blue. It matches the blue on the U.S. flag. A copper-colored star sits in the middle. This shows Arizona is the largest producer of copper in the country.

INDUSTRY

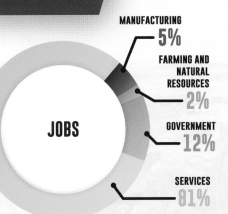

JOBS

MANUFACTURING
5%

FARMING AND NATURAL RESOURCES
2%

GOVERNMENT
12%

SERVICES
81%

Main Exports

vegetables

computer parts and electronics

copper ore   cotton   aircraft

Natural Resources
copper, turquoise, uranium, coal, silver, gold

GOVERNMENT

AZ

Federal Government
9 | 2
REPRESENTATIVES | SENATORS

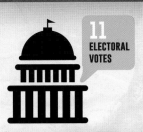

11 ELECTORAL VOTES

USA

State Government
60 | 30
REPRESENTATIVES | SENATORS

STATE SYMBOLS

STATE BIRD
CACTUS WREN

STATE MAMMAL
RINGTAIL

STATE FLOWER
SAGUARO CACTUS BLOSSOM

STATE TREE
PALO VERDE

ancestral—related to relatives who lived long ago

basin—the area drained by a river

bluffs—cliffs or steep banks that often overlook a body of water

buttes—isolated hills with steep sides

canyon—a deep and narrow valley that has steep sides

cultures—beliefs, arts, and ways of life in places or societies

flash floods—sudden floods that are over quickly; flash floods are usually caused by heavy rain or melting snow.

fry bread—a Native American flatbread made from frying dough

immigrants—people who move to a new country

manufacturing—a field of work in which people use machines to make products

missions—places where people live while spreading a religious faith

plateau—an area of flat, raised land

reservations—areas of land that are controlled by Native American tribes

rural—related to the countryside

service jobs—jobs that perform tasks for people or businesses

settled—moved somewhere and made it home

territory—an area of land under the control of a government; territories in the United States are considered part of the country but do not have power in the government.

tourism—the business of people traveling to visit other places

urban—related to cities and city life

venomous—poisonous

AT THE LIBRARY

Gregory, Josh. *Arizona*. New York, N.Y.: Children's Press, 2019.

London, Martha. *Looking into the Grand Canyon*. Mankato, Minn.: The Child's World, 2020.

Tieck, Sarah. *Arizona*. Minneapolis, Minn.: Abdo Publishing, 2020.

ON THE WEB

FACTSURFER

Factsurfer.com gives you a safe, fun way to find more information.

1. Go to www.factsurfer.com.

2. Enter "Arizona" into the search box and click Q.

3. Select your book cover to see a list of related content.

INDEX